Satellite

my guide to space exploration

Cherry Lake Press

Published in the United States of America by Cherry Lake Publishing Group
Ann Arbor, Michigan
www.cherrylakepublishing.com

Reading Adviser: Beth Walker Gambro, MS, Ed., Reading Consultant, Yorkville, IL
Book Design: Jennifer Wahi
Illustrator: Joseph Hatch

Photo Credits: NASA, 5; © Dima Zel/Shutterstock, 7; NASA, 9; NASA, 11; NASA/Serena Auñón-Chancellor, 13; NASA, 15; NASA Goddard, 17; NASA/Sultan Alneyadi, 19; NASA, 21; © Artsiom P/Shutterstock, 23

Cherry Lake Press is an imprint of Cherry Lake Publishing Group

Library of Congress Cataloging-in-Publication Data has been filed and is available at catalog.loc.gov

Printed in the United States of America

table of contents

About the author: Samantha Bell was born and raised near Orlando, Florida. She grew up in a family of eight kids and all kinds of pets, including goats, chickens, cats, dogs, rabbits, horses, parakeets, hamsters, guinea pigs, a monkey, a raccoon, and a coatimundi. She now lives with her family in the foothills of the Blue Ridge Mountains, where she enjoys hiking, painting, and snuggling with their cats Pocket, Pebble, and Mr. Tree Tree Triggers.

About the illustrator: Joseph Hatch is the art director for Tilbury House Publishers. He holds a degree in Graphic Design and Illustration from Madison College in Madison, Wisconsin. An illustrator, painter, and certified Michigan master naturalist, Joseph can usually be found at home organic gardening, beekeeping, growing edible mushrooms, planting native plants, and either building, fixing, or playing stringed instruments. He lives in Ann Arbor, Michigan, with his wife, their two children, a house cat, two dogs, nine chickens, and fifty thousand honeybees.

About Satellites

I'm a satellite. People made me. I'm in space.

Satellites **orbit** things. Some orbit the Moon. I orbit Earth.

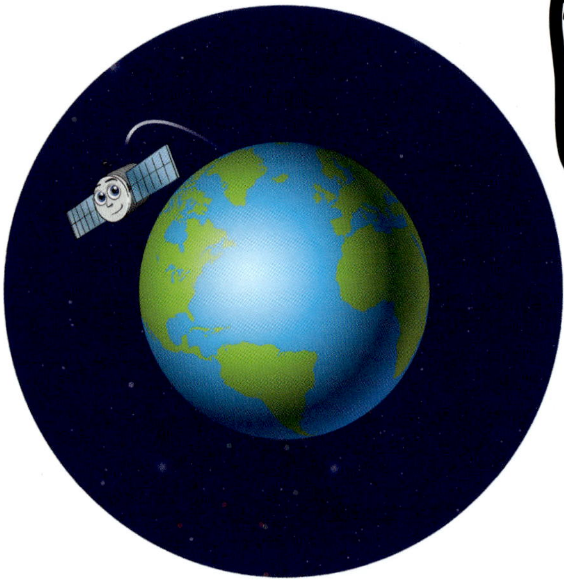

Have you seen other things with an antenna?

I have an **antenna**. It sends signals. They go to Earth. It gets signals too. They are from Earth.

I have solar arrays. They are **panels**. They use light. They turn it into **electricity**. I use it to do my job.

Satellites are not all the same. We have different jobs.

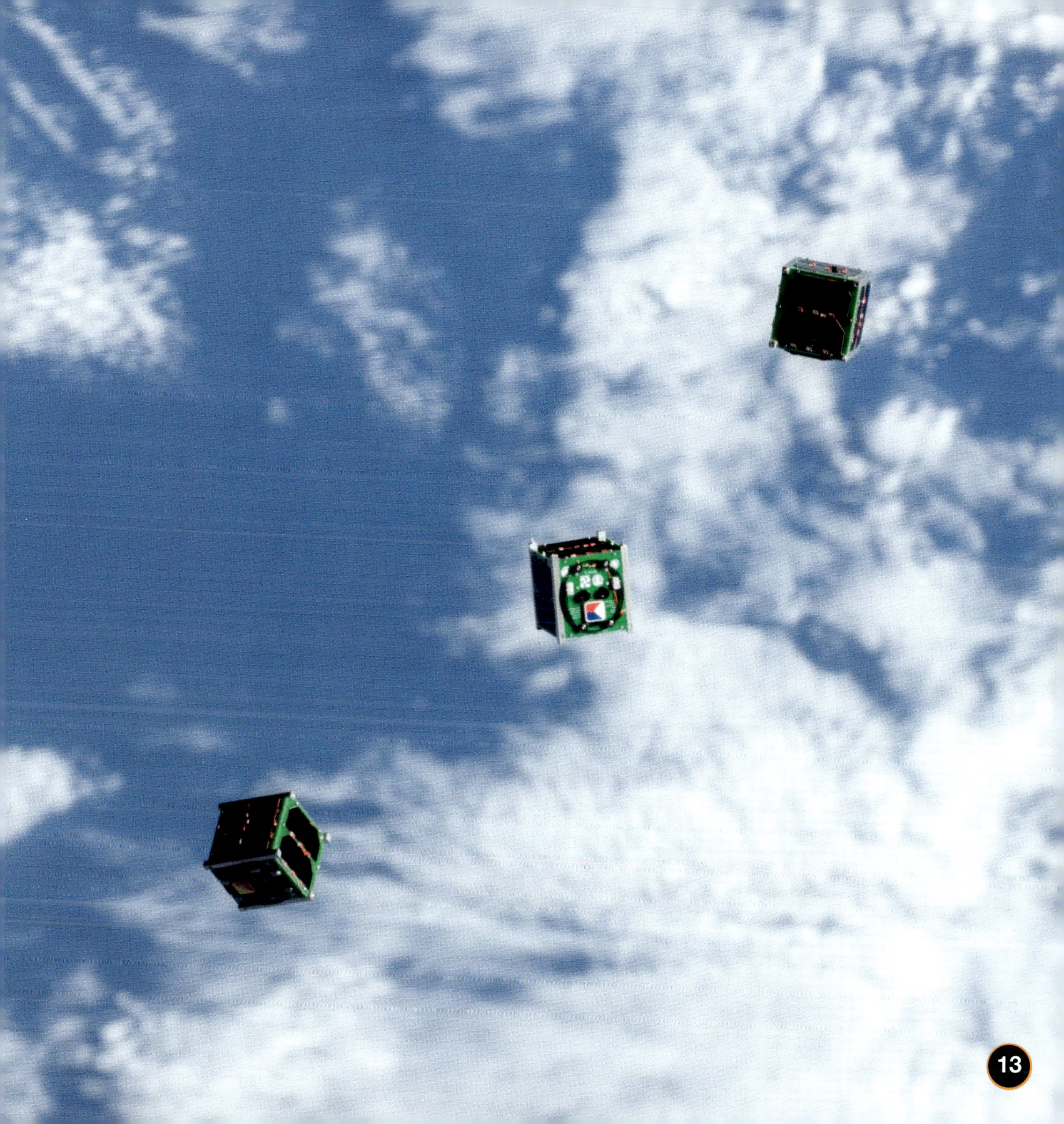

Some make phone calls.
Some send TV signals.

HUGHES

Some track weather. They take pictures. They show clouds. They show land and seas.

17

Some satellites find people.
They make **GPS** maps.

I help scientists. I help them learn. They learn about space. I have cameras. I have telescopes. I can see far. I get data. It is about stars and planets.

TRAJECTORY

I stay in space. I will stay for years!

glossary & index

glossary

antenna (an-TEH-nuh) a metal device that sends or receives radio signals

electricity (uh-lek-TRIH-suh-tee) the flow of electrical power

GPS (GEE-PEE-ESS) short for global positioning system, a system used to find a certain location on Earth

orbit (OR-buht) to revolve around something, such as planets around the Sun

panels (PAA-nuhlz) a separate part of a surface

telescopes (TEH-luh-skohps) instruments that use lenses or mirrors to make distant objects appear larger

index